STYLE
COMFORT
HOME

STYLE
COMFORT
HOME

How to Find Your Style and
Decorate for Happiness and Ease

Andrew Howard
Written with Andrew Sessa

Abrams, New York

For my wife, Katie, our kids, Jack and Henry,
and my parents. You taught me everything I know, and
I still learn from each of you all day, every day.

CONTENTS

INTRODUCTION

When I was a kid, growing up in Jacksonville, Florida, we had furniture in our house that my three siblings and I had to pay a five dollar fine for sitting in. Some of my brothers and sisters somehow managed to hold on to their money, and pretty tightly, too, but our parents used to have to fine me again and again . . . and again.

Back then, I didn't know I'd grow up to be a designer, even though my parents were in the business. But I *did* know that when I had a house of my own, I'd make sure it was free of furniture that came with a five dollar fine.

A decade-plus later, I graduated from college, moving out of a dorm with a bunch of junk furniture that I ended up just throwing away. I figured there had to be a better way—something between those fancy five dollar–fine pieces I grew up with and all that disposable undergraduate stuff I couldn't wait to get rid of.

Since then, I've made my design career all about helping young families find that space in between. Together, we create rooms that are as approachable, as comfortable, and above all else, as *livable* as they are lovely to look at. With an assist from me and my studio, folks learn how to turn their personal style and the way they live right now into a personalized way of decorating. That lets us create houses that feel like home.

And that feeling is important, because home is way more than the place you rest your head. It's where you watch your kids grow up, where you put your Christmas tree, where you have all those amazing family dinners. A happy, great-looking house is a direct reflection of you, the people who live there. Everyone deserves a great home, and everyone can have one. It will evolve over time, to be sure—taking care of a house is a lot like taking care of yourself—but I want you to know that it is something you can achieve.

With this book, I'll show you how to create a home for your family that is inviting, timeless, and entirely your own. I'm here to tell you that you can get that, no matter your budget, no matter your style, no matter how crazy your family may be.

I've got a crazy family, too—and not just my parents with their furniture fines and my siblings. My wife and I have two high-energy boys of our own, and through the years we've had our share of dogs, cats, and other animals of various stripes. We know what crazy looks like.

True to my childhood vision from all those years back, there's not a single piece of five dollar–fine furniture in our house. Instead, we've managed to make spaces for ourselves that balance the practical with the beautiful, and you absolutely can, too. I can't wait to show you how.

PART ONE

HOW WE LIVE NOW
Defining Your Style

Finding the right look for your house comes down to two things: your personal style and your lifestyle. If you dress conservatively, you'll likely want to decorate that way, and if you don't own any pink clothes, you can probably skip the rose curtains. As for lifestyle, ask yourself how your family lives—and answer honestly! Do you entertain formally or casually . . . or not at all? Are you neat or messy? Do you spend time together or apart? Next, check out pictures on Instagram, Pinterest, and in magazines. You'll quickly start gravitating toward certain designs and away from others. Here, we'll look at the styles the families I work with love the most. They're loose categories to be sure, and conveniently, they blend into one another. They also leave plenty of room for personalization, making it easy to find yourself in these rooms.

You deserve a home that's a stylish reflection of you, your family, and your unique personal style.
I know that sounds sort of self-helpy, but it's true. All it takes are some interesting design features, favorite objects, original artwork, and fun accents. These lattice-covered walls are an unexpected surprise, one that plays well with the wicker furniture, mix of whimsical prints, and just-bold-enough palette.

1. New Formal

If the *old* formal was my parents' house filled with the sort of swanky furniture I had to pay a five dollar fine for sitting in, the new formal leaves room for fun. It's more overstuffed than stuffy, more fanciful than fancy. And it's forgiving, too. In today's world, where so many of us feel like we're working too hard for too long every day, all we want is to just be comfortable and ourselves at home. And that's true even if you like traditional lines and a tailored look. The new formal lets us enjoy our homes without being held captive by any prim and proper stiffness. It allows for nicks in the coffee table, cookie crumbs, and red wine spills. (Stain-proof outdoor fabrics are major indoor assets.) There's a certain structure to the look, with cleaner lines, solid colors, and rich textures, but unlike the formal design of decades past, it allows for plenty of your own personality to shine through.

Got a space with a showstopping architectural element? Work *with* it, never against it.

If you have something in your home as statement-making as this sweeping formal staircase, remember you're lucky. In this foyer, the subtlety of the spare furnishings, the geometric floor pattern, and the wall paneling's straight lines let the stairs enjoy the spotlight.

Good news: The days of all-white trim are over.
Colorful trim is where it's at. For a more formal look, keep moldings a bit darker than the walls. You can find the right hue by going a few shades down on the color strip from the paint shop. You'll create the perfect combo.

Forget what your mom told you when you learned to dress yourself. Most colors don't clash.

Two shades of the same or similar colors—a certain red with a certain maroon, say—may not look right together. But when you combine hues from across the color wheel, you're golden. Just look at this plum-and-aqua dining room. The unexpected, high-contrast palette proved just the thing to transform a traditional space.

18

When figuring out a room's color scheme, a carpet is a good place to start.

An area rug can point you to the perfect palette, especially if you already have a carpet you love or if you find one early in the design process. Pulling from its hues to select fabric and paint colors is a classic trick. It works in rooms new and old, formal and informal. Solids and small-scale patterns get along especially well with larger rugs.

This isn't your parents' old-school guest bedroom. Instead, it breaks just enough of the traditional rules to live squarely in the present day. The classic lines of its furniture, the mostly pale neutral palette, and yes, the hunting dog art give it a certain formality, but the mix of darker masculine hues and plaids with feminine pastels and florals, as well as the swing-arm sconce, sisal carpet, and painted nightstand, keep things fresh.

Little rooms, especially bedrooms, can be tricky, but you can still live large and stylishly in them.
When space is tight, skip the table lamps in favor of something wall-mounted. That'll let you have a smaller nightstand and give you more open area on the floor. You wouldn't usually put a bed and bedside table this close to the bathroom door, but doing so here lets the bed face a window on the opposite wall.

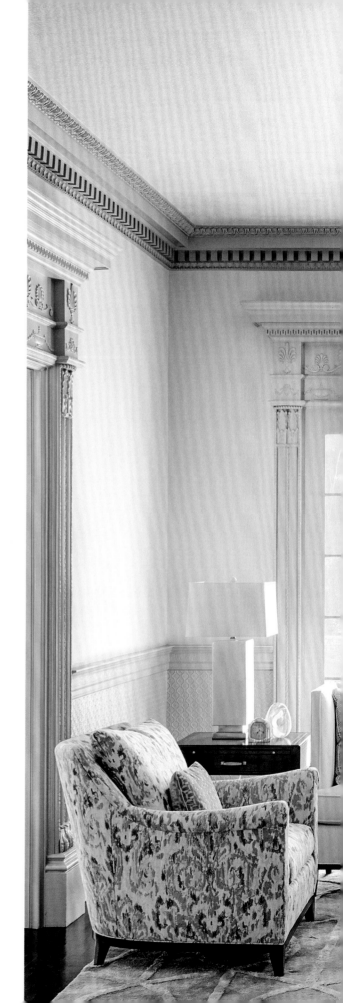

In a room with traditional formality to spare, change things up to make it more modern.

Crown moldings! Wainscoting! Columned windows with complex capitals! This room had it all. So much so that it was almost too much. To tone it down, we painted the ornamentation a pale pink and the walls a light gray, adding a subtly printed wallpaper to the ceiling. Contemporary furnishings complete the new-meets-old look.

No room for a sofa? Create comfort with armchairs around an ottoman.

This can be your new go-to furniture arrangement in tight quarters. It has the softness and potential for color and pattern that come with upholstery, plus the flexibility of petite pieces that can be moved around to do double duty. That sort of easy-flexi aspect puts the "new" in "new formal."

Make the place you sleep as soothing and restful as possible.
I get it. It's your personal space, and few people see it. But I'd discourage you from leaving it undecorated or from going wild. I like neutral tones and lots of soft textures, but your bedroom is your sanctuary. Whatever Zen looks like for you, go for it.

2. Modern Relaxed

You want a relaxed house to feel like the opposite of a stressful day. So, the furniture that fills it absolutely has to be comfortable. These days, we need spaces that are as cozy, welcoming, soft, and easy as possible. I don't know about you, but I'd rather not come home every night to find my family fighting over the one comfy spot in the living room or trying to figure out how to remove yet another stain from that all-too-precious upholstery. But that doesn't mean we need to stuff our houses with huge vinyl sectionals and beanbag chairs, either—no matter how much our kids want us to. Instead, look for gentle curves, fluffy throw pillows, finishes that age well as they get nicked and dinged, and different seating options that will encourage good conversation and let everyone sit comfortably during a long movie. The trick is in finding a mix of pieces that are as functional, friendly, and good to live with as they are nice to look at.

To make a large living space welcoming and comfortable, divide it into multiple seating areas.
There's nothing relaxing about a cavernous-looking room, especially one with too few pieces of furniture or those selected just for their size. Here's a better way: Choose human-scaled items and use them to create a few conversation-friendly arrangements. This lets a big room be intimate, even when just two people are in it.

Weave some common threads between two rooms that open to one another.

The spaces don't have to match—it's better if they don't, actually. But elements that bring color and texture from one room to the next make for good transitions and keep things cohesive. Here, the blue from the kitchen backsplash carries into the family room, whose cane coffee table echoes the counter stools.

When you have space for just one piece of furniture in your foyer, go for a bench with an open base and clean lines.

Console tables are nice, but you can't sit on them, so they don't help you put shoes on. A chest offers storage space, but it can look heavy. A bench is light on its feet—and family friendly. My sons use ours all the time. OPPOSITE: A banquette-style corner sofa combines comfortable seating and a small footprint.

Lacquered walls brighten a space. They're an easy way to throw light around.

"Lacquer" sounds kind of fancy, but it doesn't have to be. High-gloss paint looks just right in relaxed spaces, especially in light colors. Hues are always brighter in real life, so pick a paint chip a bit grayer than what you're after. And remember: Paler walls look better with furniture in more saturated hues.

Comfort is key, especially in smaller gathering and seating spaces.
Be on the lookout for unusual antique chairs or stools that add visual interest, but when you're short on space, let comfort be your guide. What mattered most in this great room was that everyone in the family had somewhere cozy to sit— and enough room on the coffee table for their drinks (and their feet, too).

If your family's like mine, you may find that the idea of a formal dining room is often more theoretical than practical. Our dining room table has served as a craft corner, a homework hot zone, and even a makeshift fort. That's why I love flexible spaces like this breakfast area, which is open to a kitchen and becomes a de facto dining room. It's designed to blur the lines and welcome all—exactly what a relaxed house needs.

Easily washed, tough, and durable, indoor-outdoor rugs are the way to go in family eating areas.
I learned the hard way that even some outdoor fabrics are no match for kids and a slice of pizza. My boys can destroy an entire carpet with one piece each—maybe even one split between them, if there's pepperoni. When you use a rug in an eat-in kitchen or breakfast room, you need to be able to just take it outside and literally hose it off. Trust me.

Change pillows—or even just their covers—to completely transform a space.

Swapping out your throw pillows every few years, or even each season, brings in new hues. It's a great way to dip your toe into color, if you're afraid of going all in. Here, the neutral backdrop of the furnishings and fittings makes it especially easy.

All-white kitchens are all about their accessories—and a single splash of color.

I like a clean, simple cooking space as much as anyone, and nothing looks cleaner or simpler than white. But to keep things interesting—and welcoming—a kitchen needs a little bit more. Add a colored backsplash, then try some statement seating and interesting lighting over the island. Done and done.

Sometimes—maybe even most of the time—you can find your palette right outside your window.

I know it seems almost too easy to use the color scheme that nature gives you. But, like arguing with a toddler who just wants to go down the slide one more time, there's really no reason to fight it. The idea here was to complement the ocean outside and draw the eye to the view. Rich blues and low-slung furniture keep the focus on the water.

Remember to leave room for a getting-ready zone, somewhere to put on make-up, clothes, and shoes.
Sometimes these spots will be at the foot of the bed, sometimes in a walk-in closet or dressing room. These days, they're appearing in bathrooms, too. Create an area to do make-up by dropping a vanity down by six inches, to desk height, and adding a chair, or put a counter stool at the regular height.

3. Contemporary Bohemian

Back in the day, people designed period rooms, with furnishings all from one era or aesthetic. These spaces looked good, but they were also, well, boring. Now, thankfully, things are much less buttoned-up. Good style today means creating an eclectic mix—which is a much better way to express your own personality and interests. That's especially true of this contemporary bohemian vibe. It combines global influences, rich textures, bold patterns, undulating lines, and often-surprising materials, resulting in rooms that have a collected look, as if you put them together over the years, adding pieces from your travels. They're curated, but casual about it. Part of the fun here is the endless room for interpretation, and the accessories that you can switch in and out seasonally or over time. No two bohemian rooms should look the same—something that's true even if they're in the same house.

Mix in antique furnishings to make a room feel complete—and to add an on-point dose of the eclectic.
Even if everything in a space was bought new and installed all at once, you want your design to look like it came together over time as you acquired different things. Vintage pieces help achieve that—and they're so much fun to look for. We found the blue chair here at a thrift store in Connecticut and the garden seat at one in North Carolina.

Rugs in a room don't have to match—especially when they define different spaces.

In this open living and dining room, the color palettes of the two carpets are virtually the same, but the scales of their patterns change things up. The rug in the eating area has a very small and whimsical motif, while the one in the sitting area is larger scaled and more geometric. Instead of competing, they complement each other, and that makes the room more interesting.

Feel free to mix bold patterns with abandon—but remember to add neutrals, too.

If you're planning to put a lot of big prints together in a room, lay out everything you're considering and look at it all together. Make sure the scales (big vs. small) and the styles (geometric vs. painterly) vary. Then, be sure to give yourself some calm space—maybe it's plain white walls, maybe a simple gray-washed table, maybe a neutral sofa.

Low stools at a cocktail table save space and provide extra seating in a pinch. When you have people over, a living room that's usually used by two or four people becomes a space for eight, ten . . . twenty. Petite seats can be subtly tucked away, then moved out and around when and where they're needed. The rush tops of the ones shown here work well with the Turkish ikat on the armchairs, the red pillow, and the geometric blue-and-white carpet.

Matchy-matchy can be great. Too matchy-matchy, though? Not so great.

If you're not super comfortable mixing a lot of different big prints together, a good way to let yourself experiment with pattern is to find one bold fabric you love and then use it in just a few different ways in a room. Here, the fun floral from the floor-to-ceiling curtains gets repeated on the armchair, while almost everything else remains solid.

Color can serve as a source of light and warmth as much as sunshine does.
I won't lie. This yellow sofa had me a little nervous. But it makes the room. Often, the decisions we lose sleep over turn out best. In this case, the yellow proved to be the perfect pairing with the citrus print and blue-and-green kitchen tile.

Every room starts with something. This one began with the homeowner's vintage rug and her love for mixing pattern and color. We pulled brighter hues from the carpet for the bold and variously scaled prints of the curtains, sofa, and pillows, then balanced all that big energy with some quieter neutrals.

Remember: You're decorating your house for you, not for anyone else.
That's always true, even if you're hiring an interior designer. I always want a room to be a reflection of its residents and their style, not a reflection of me. Here, we worked with the homeowner's prized poufs, black-and-white photographs, and vintage carpet—as well as her desire for a grapefruit-colored sofa—adding in items that felt of a piece with her personal possessions and passions.

Guest rooms give you a chance to break the mold of the rest of your house and go for a little extra drama.

I've had people call my guest room (OPPOSITE) "Busy." And that's fine, because they're usually the same folks who I call "People I Don't Want Staying in My House All That Long, Anyway." Guest rooms should show off a little bit; they're definitely not the place to just put the leftover college furniture you don't know what else to do with and hope no one notices.

PART TWO

READY, SET, DECORATE
Getting Started

Figuring out *where* to begin designing often means determining *what* to begin with. You can base an entire room on a beloved series of art, a prized piece of furniture, or an amazing rug you already own. If you don't have something to build around, start by selecting the carpet or a "lead" fabric—a large print you see as the star of the show. Pull your color palette from that, then select coordinating fabrics in different scales. Next, give your room a collected look: Select wooden pieces from various eras if they're vintage, always with complementary, as opposed to matching, finishes and lines. Then layer in accessories, including art, pillows, and lamps. Finding the right mix takes care, but it's fun, too. We'll get into all of this in much more detail in the following sections, which are all about helping you successfully design a room's various pieces and parts.

Seeking inspiration? Try looking up! The vaulted beamed ceiling of this room provided a jumping-off point.
It immediately created a light and lively atmosphere, something we continued in the colors, the furniture, and the materials of this family room. The color palette extends the airy atmosphere, while the earthy textures of the woven-rope chair and seagrass rug serve to ground the space.

1. Hitting the Ceiling

You heard it here first, folks: The ceiling is officially the fifth wall of any room in your house. Not only that, but it's usually the most important wall, too. Why? The ceiling, more than any other surface, *defines* your space. For that reason alone, it deserves your attention. But it also demands consideration because ceilings just have so much darn potential to become real showstoppers. The biggest mistake people make is simply leaving them blank. Blank is blah, as far as I'm concerned. Instead, think about all the tools you have in your toolkit for walls—paint, wallpaper, fabric, upholstery, decorative finishes, lacquer, beams, paneling—and then pick one or two to deploy up above. Colors and materials that contrast or blend with what's happening down below can both work, and a statement light fixture is always a hit. Have no fear: I'll walk you through everything to make sure you don't get in over your head.

Great ceilings make for great rooms. And great ceiling fixtures—whether contemporary or traditional, hung high or low—make for even better ones.
The monumental, whitewashed wooden ceiling trusses of this family room set the neutral tone for the entire space. The height here really could have hindered a sense of warmth, but the amount of sunlight and the palette of browns, taupes, and tans keep the heat turned up (even when paired with icier blues). The dramatic brass chandelier helps a ton, too.

Mix and match materials and textures to create a statement ceiling.

Ceilings are usually kept all one color so they don't become a distraction. But here, we needed to do more to get the vintage look we were after. The neutral, low-contrast palette of the new painted beams and salvaged tongue-and-groove boards keeps this ceiling just subtle enough, even as it adds a layer of texture that's right at home in this beach house.

Pair darker furnishings with a pastel ceiling and light furnishings with a dark one.

Most rooms have pale-colored ceilings, to make them seem taller. The lightness above allows you to work with more saturated colors in your decorating below. But sometimes you'll find you want a dark ceiling—to make a too-high room seem more intimate, for example. If that's the case, it's usually best to keep things light at floor level.

Carry a statement ceiling's color down into the trim in the rest of the room.

For the sake of continuity—and because I just thought it would look so darn good—I used the same color on the doors here that I had used up above. It's dark, to be sure, but it works well against the otherwise all-white expanse of the walls and their trim. The wrought iron curtain rod provides another nice dark accent.

Can't find antique beams the right size for your ceiling? Just fake 'em.

Old wood gives some great warmth and a sense of importance to a space. It lets a room look like it's stood the test of time—even if it's newly built and the materials only *look* vintage.

That's the case here. We painted new white pine with watered-down shades of brown, gray, and cream that let the grain show through.

When it comes to adding embellishment to your ceiling, more is very often more.

Your walls may have a lot going on, but that's no reason to overlook the ceiling—think of it as icing on the cake. Even if the cake and filling are delicious, everyone loves the frosting, right? Here, I sized the honeycomb pattern to make sure I ended up with a clean, organized look, without any odd bits of hexagon around the edges. This room, which is in my own home, ended up being the classroom for my first grader during the homeschooling days of 2020. His friends all agreed the ceiling was cool, so I guess I did something right.

Dining room design is all about ambiance—creating the perfect setting for all sorts of meals, whether celebratory or romantic, formal or casual, intimate or overflowing. Whatever a room's style and size, I love a ceiling with a sense of sparkle in these sorts of spaces. It's just the thing for bouncing candlelight all around. And nothing does sparkle better than a wallpaper with a bit of shimmer or sheen. I know you're thinking, "You want me to wallpaper my ceiling?" To which I can only say, "Yeah, you'll thank me later!"

More than almost anything else, wallpaper turns a ceiling into the focal point of a room. You'll find it's a total game changer.
Nothing lets a ceiling become a room's focal point and truly its fifth wall like wallpaper. Using it gives the eyes something to take in where there's often a blank space, and in a way that's easier (and less expensive) to achieve than paneling or beams. Typically, I like something with a pattern in a relatively small scale, so the motif doesn't get overwhelming on the whole ceiling.

Grade-school geometry is all you need to design even the most complicated of ceilings.

Ok. Full disclosure: When the carpenter showed up to construct and install the beams for this ceiling, he said "you gotta be kidding me" no fewer than ten times when looking at my drawing. But the top pattern is just a series of octagons, which then led to the rectangles and trapezoids below. Come on! It's sixth-grade stuff, max . . .

Looking to bring a little bit of the outdoors in?
Try a latticework ceiling and green accents.

Some folks are resistant to lattice, because they're worried about dusting it. But when you use a satin-finish paint, dust shouldn't stick. This room is in my own house, and I can tell you we haven't had a problem. Also, my kids loved playing with the lattice strips like they were Lincoln Logs when we were getting ready to install them, which made the whole thing worth it.

2. Working All Four Walls

Every great space requires a good floor plan. But while it's called a *floor* plan, the fact is, where and how you place your furniture is actually more about the walls than it is the floor. The floor is bounded by those walls, after all, so you have to think about them when figuring out where to place furniture, even before you know exactly what every piece will look like. You'll want to anchor a bed or sofa against a certain wall, for example, or center a dining table in a room between a pair of windows or align it with an arched opening. When it comes to treating those walls, I encourage you to have some fun. Paint is just the tip of the iceberg. Wood paneling, upholstery, textured papers, hand-created murals, mirrors, moldings, and fine art all work wonders and add tons of character.

If paneled walls aren't in the budget, use pieces of wooden trim to give yourself the look for less.
This is a great way to create the appearance of paneling without having to bring in—or pay for—the panels. In this case, we painted the trim two different hues to pick up on the room's warmer and cooler gray tones. When doing a wall treatment like this, I always lay out the furniture first and then make sure the paneling or trim sits centered on the other pieces in the room.

Pick a subtle accent hue to color coordinate your walls and ceiling.

As an additional easy-to-execute detail, I'll often glaze the inset molding of wall panels with watered-down paint to really set them off and emphasize their three-dimensional quality. I usually pick one of the paler tones that's already in the room for this, and here, as an added bonus, I used the same color for the ceiling.

Think of a plain, empty room as a blank canvas. The lack of design elements may seem daunting, but it doesn't have to be if you consider it an opportunity to introduce a bit of embellishment, understated or otherwise. Here, a geometric grasscloth wallpaper and wainscoting give what had been a generic white box of a dining room some much needed—but still subtle—oomph. The combination of patterns and textures helps the neutral palette come alive.

Mix materials to make a room appear as if it evolved organically over time.

Nothing makes a room look as impersonal as overly coordinated décor. Materials don't all have to match, and things will actually look better if they don't. In this space, the nickel chandelier, gilt lamps, and brass hardware create a collected feeling, as if the folks who live here found different pieces they loved and kept updating the space.

Unless you're hosting state dinners, lacquered walls usually look best with simpler paneling.
High-gloss paints are great, especially in rooms that have only one window or otherwise don't get a lot of sun. The sheen of the finish bounces light all over the space. When you're going the lacquer route, though, remember that the walls don't have to be particularly embellished in any other way. This room works well because the paneling is pretty spare.

**Hand-painted wallpaper is an absolute luxury,
one worth finding funds for in your budget if you can.**

I'm going to go out on a limb here and say this: If you can afford hand-painted
wallpaper, you should have it. It's such a conversation starter and showpiece.
The tree design here is what's called "naïve," which means it looks like a silhouette.
It's perfect for a room you want to give a less-formal atmosphere.

Add wainscoting to help vertical stripes make a room look just tall enough—and never too tall.

I love stripes. Can't get enough of them, actually. Stripes are so timeless, they have never gone out of style, and they never will. We use them today nonstop, and we see them in houses that have been around for hundreds and hundreds of years, too. This wainscoting trick is stolen from some of those historical homes, in fact. The expanse of solid green at the bottom of the wall grounds the room, while the stripes lift the ceiling.

How to make outdoor spaces special? Incorporate elements that would look at home inside, too.

The shingled walls here are almost the only sign that these spaces are alfresco. The furnishings and design details are otherwise lifted from interior design. At my house, we tell the kids it's "Captain's Hour" at around 8:30 PM, and they go inside and leave us adults alone. A friend coined the term with his children, and it works surprisingly well.

Wood-paneled rooms are always a favorite—even when you achieve the look without any actual panels.

Getting the appearance of wood paneling doesn't have to break your budget. In the room above, we used strips of molding to frame a grid right on top of the drywall, then painted it all one color, so it seemed like we hung panels. It's harder to fake the unpainted knotty pine room shown opposite, though you can find wallpapers that come close.

Use plaster on walls to add a layer of texture that you can't quite get any other way.
The material offers a little bit of shimmer and a whole lot of mottling, and it warms up a space in a way that painted drywall just doesn't. It also makes every wall in your house unique. When the plaster is applied by hand, the process leaves each inch of wall space ever so slightly different than the next. And as seen here, it's a great backdrop for bold art.

INSTANT GALLERY WALL Although frequently added as a finishing touch, art is among a room's most important elements. But don't worry: As these examples illustrate, it doesn't have to be precious to be perfect. What matters is the art's meaning to you and its ability to elevate a space.

Sometimes, the simplest solutions are found in your own two hands, or, in this case, in *my* own hand. When we couldn't find the exact sort of geometric artwork we wanted to complement the curving lines of the desk chair, I just went ahead and drew something out myself. We had it framed up, and there you have it: an easy, and inexpensive, focal point.

RIGHT: I like to try to find art in everything, anywhere I can. For this dining room, I framed the homeowner's beloved Hermès scarf, one of many in her collection, and hung it over a mid-century sideboard. She loved it.

ABOVE: When designing a gallery wall, I always work out the configuration and spacing on the floor first. The key is to make the arrangement look like it grew naturally over time, starting with two or three anchor pieces and expanding from there.

LEFT: For art placed above a stained piece of wood furniture, I like to use a frame in a contrasting stain or even a brighter color if the wall is neutral. As for the art here, I love how the loose lines provide a counterpoint to the cabinet's gridded look.

3. Letting in Light

Natural light is almost always your friend—*except* for those early mornings when you've been up too late the night before enjoying yourself a little too much with friends. And then your four-year-old bounds into your room pretending to be Spiderman and throws open all the curtains. But, even then, rooms flooded with sun are just the best. They seem bigger, friendlier, more welcoming, and more fun. When designing a house from the ground-up, make sure you have windows on two sides of every room, if you can. If you don't have that flexibility, there's still lots you can do with creative placement of mirrors and art. Then, use curtains, shades, and blinds to create privacy and block light when you need to. (Remember those early mornings?) Window treatments can also frame views, telling the eye where to land, and they soften walls with color, pattern, and print. Aside from a room whose whole point is its windows, spaces without curtains will almost always look like something is missing.

**If curtains or shades aren't part of your plan,
painted window frames can be a great stand-in.**
The architecture of this high-ceilinged, octagonal room is all about its windows and the framing around them. Covering that up with curtains or shades seemed like it would be a shame. So instead, we added color by painting the windows themselves, in a shade of blue that would complement the furniture, especially the similar hues in the sofa.

When it comes to pairing curtains with French doors, combine form and function.

It's not a written-in-stone rule, but I always like to hang curtains that can be opened and closed, even if they're for French doors that people use to walk in and out of. It may be tempting—and it's certainly cheaper—to just hang some stationary fabric panels to frame the glass, but you'll appreciate having operable curtains to create privacy and block the sun, especially if your room faces south or west.

Hang curtains and shades a bit higher than your windows to accentuate a room's height.

Even if you're blessed with tall ceilings, it almost never hurts to emphasize that fact. For the curtains over the large window here, we hung the rod just below the crown molding (whose color—no accident—matches the fabric of the window treatments). As for the Roman shades flanking the headboard, their placement above the windows' upper molding also adds some lift.

Bold window treatment fabrics are great at taking the lead without stealing the show.

Because they open and close, curtains and shades are great spots to deploy a room's "lead" fabric—the relatively bold textile that helps you design your color and pattern palette. When closed, they won't overwhelm, no matter how wild the print, and when they're open, they make for a fun reveal.

In a glass-walled room, the trick is to control the sun even as you let it in.
This can be done with window treatments inside, of course, but many people don't realize you can also do something outside to help. In this house, the architecture includes a wide overhang at the top of the windows, which has the benefit of shading the room. If your home wasn't built similarly, this is an effect you could create with awnings or a pergola. Curtains, of course, continue to remain a good move, both for the sake of privacy and for limiting the sun even more.

Use curtains and shades in the same room for a decorating one-two punch.

Hanging different kinds of treatments on several windows in a single space is a winning design strategy. It lets you save space when you need to—as it did here, where there was no room for hanging curtains on either side of the window next to the bed—and it allows you to show off the same fabric in various ways. The shades spotlight what the print looks like when laid flat or pulled up in pleats, while the curtains reveal a more flowing look.

When in Rome, do as the Romans do:
Use Roman shades over a sofa and next to a bed.

OK, so that's not really a rule of classical Italian decorating, but it's good advice. Curtains are hard to open and close behind a sofa, and they get all bunched up next to a headboard. Shades maintain privacy without having fabric interfere with furnishings.

For a crisp and finished look, place shades inside your window frames.

There's a bit of a trade-off to figure out when hanging bedroom window treatments. Putting them above the top of window trim lets you block more sun, but putting them below gives you a more tailored appearance. It all sort of depends on how light-sensitive you are. Here, we split the difference, hanging the curtains high and the shades low.

Layer room-darkening and sheer curtains to adjust natural light to your liking.

In a bedroom, there's no better way to treat your windows—and yourself—than by hanging a heavy drape to block the sun in the morning over a sheer that'll let in light but still ensure privacy when you're not trying to sleep. Keep in mind: To make this work, you'll need to put up a double curtain rod, so the two layers can move independently.

INSTANT WINDOW SEATS It's hard to find a spot that's sweeter than a window seat. These cozy, comfortable crowd-pleasers take advantage of sun and views like nothing else. Best of all, they appeal equally to kids and parents alike. I've yet to meet someone who doesn't love them.

There's much more to window seats than cushioned banquette-style spots where you can sit or lie down with a good book. Those are great, don't get me wrong. But a desk built into a natural sun–filled alcove also accomplishes some super-efficient space savings—and turns working from home into a joy. Here, we reclaimed some space in a bedroom by reorganizing the floor plan of an adjacent bathroom. Rather than turning it into a second closet, which the room didn't need, we took advantage of the round window to make a lovely little contemplative zone. The large rectangles of the wallpaper's pattern offer a subtle nod to windowpanes while also providing contrast to the circular opening.

RIGHT: This desk setup, next to a low-ceilinged area in a top-floor bedroom, makes the most of a spot that might have ended up as squandered space. The verdant wall color and botanical-print curtains combine with wicker-and-rattan furniture for a vibrant indoor-outdoor feel.

ABOVE: When you're designing a window seat, think about bringing the view inside. The watery hues here echo the colors of the river outside. Classically detailed bookshelves, meanwhile, make this little sanctuary a dream of a book nook.

LEFT: Window seats in kids' rooms are a real perk. They're perfect for storytime fun, and they create space for built-in baskets, bookshelves, and cubbies—offering quick cleanup solutions for stowing stuff when guests are coming.

4. Decorating in Color

The freedom to be as colorful as you like is one of the best parts about decorating your home. But how do you start? First, try finding something to base your color scheme on: a piece of art you have or you know you'll get for a room; a fabric you've totally fallen for that you want to give a starring role; a carpet, heirloom or otherwise, that will lay the groundwork for all that goes above and around it. From there, if wall coverings aren't in your budget, many of the most important color choices you'll make will be about paint. Changing wall and trim colors will have more dramatic impact than any of the furniture choices you make—which is nice, because paint is one of the easier, and cheaper, things to change in a room. Try to stay away from trendy hues, and don't always think you have to be bold. There's nothing wrong with a quiet, subtle scheme.

Fear the monotony of monochrome? Add neutrals to a scheme based on different shades of a single color.
I use blue constantly, in every shade, sometimes in the same space. But an all-blue room can be too much of a good thing. Here, the slightly distressed natural finish of the wooden pieces breaks up the rhapsody in blue. An added bonus: The rush side chairs give kids a place to sit where grubby hands won't stain upholstery.

Remember: It takes (only) two to tango. Try a palette that pairs just a couple of bold hues together.

The tennis-ball yellow shade of the dining chairs increases this room's style factor, while the fact that it's an outdoor fabric ensures it is kid friendly. Combining the color with a bright blue creates a great combo—their similar degree of saturation ensures that they set each other off nicely.

Outdoor fabrics let a room take a licking and keep on ticking.
This is the living room in my own home, where my boys like to jump from the cocktail table to the sofas with a juice box in one hand and cheese puffs in the other. The textiles, designed for alfresco use, stay unstained, and the white-painted wood walls are easy to wipe down.

**To make sure your bold art remains the main event,
limit the rest of your palette to mostly pale neutrals.**

Light-colored earth tones, ivories, and whites allow interesting, colorful art to stand out
as the star of the decorating show. If you use brightly hued furniture, textiles, rugs,
and wall and window treatments, your works could be relegated to playing a bit part.

You'd never know by looking at it, but when this room was first finished, the family used it almost exclusively for their young daughter to play, letting her run laps around the table with her hobbyhorse. As they settled in and she settled down, it became a spot for more adult, but still animated, activities: convivial dinners and joyful conversation. That's the great thing about a colorful scheme like this. It plays well with all ages.

Combine pink and blue for a palette that's not feminine or masculine, but instead at a sweet spot in between.
Sure, we're a long way from the days when pink was just for girls and blue was just for boys. (My sons are happy to wear the sweetest of pastels for Easter.) But the colors do still have their connotations. I like to put them together in rooms that should have universal appeal, like this family-friendly dining room.

Be fearless with color—especially when it comes to the paint for your walls. Changing it is easy.

Some of the hardest conversations I ever have with people are about yellow walls. I'm not sure why, but certain colors can be scary for folks—or at least out of their comfort zones. But here's the thing about paint: It's not forever. Hate it? Change it. For what it's worth, though, yellow always makes me happy.

**Any way you do it—and anywhere—blue just works.
Big or small, bright or dark, up or down, and side to side.**

Whether used only as an accent or as the color that clads an entire room, blue is a great go-to. This bathroom plays with two tones of the same shade—one lighter, one darker. OPPOSITE: This den shows blue off in saturated ways: on the lacquered walls and the armchair as well as in the pattern of the sofa and the wallpaper on the ceiling.

INSTANT PASTEL PERFECTION Pastel hues are happy—the colors of spring, of youth, of fun. They're the easiest way I know to brighten up a room. Pick one with a bit of gray in it to make sure it's not *too* bright. And beware of using too many pastels together; I call that the rainbow sherbet trap.

People love a pale-blue bedroom, and I get why. Few things are quite as soothing when it comes to sleep. (Maybe a paint company should market a color like this called "Melatonin"?) Here, in a room with an otherwise natural and neutral palette, I selected a coverlet almost the exact same shade of blue as the walls, which really pulls the whole thing together. Pairing the two provides extra interest and a pretty glow, without letting the hue become overwhelming.

RIGHT: A palette of pastels, like this one, can start to feel a little too juvenile or sweet, so unless you're designing for a unicorn (or a unicorn-obsessed kiddo), find colors with earthier brown and gray tones in them.

ABOVE: Folks often worry they'll get tired of a colored backsplash, but I always tell them they're more likely to get bored of a white one than tired of a colored one. I haven't been proven wrong yet. Doing a light, watery glaze like this gives you just enough color.

LEFT: You often see tongue-and-groove paneling painted white, but that's hardly the only option. This light blue-green turned out to be just the thing for a small family room. White would've been stark, but this is warm and welcoming, despite being a cool color.

**Pink is timeless—and ageless. Sure, little girls love it.
But no one says you have to grow out of it.**

When the owner of this home said she wanted a pink closet, I was thrilled. For me, because what could be more fun than designing a pink closet? But also for her, because pink provides a soft glow that makes everyone look better—just what you want when you're getting ready to go out. OPPOSITE: Pink and white, plus aqua and mint, feel just right.

Combine pastels with neutrals other than white to warm them up and help them mature.

This bedroom's beiges and browns work with pinks to keep the space cozy even on cold days. While we're here, I should tell you: I love twin beds. I grew up sleeping in one while sharing a room with my brother, and my boys do the same. I'll always remember those late-night conversations about all kinds of different things.

144

In children's rooms, subtlety can—and usually should—be thrown out the window.

I always tell folks to pick shades lighter than what they think they want, not because I don't trust them, but because colors in a real room tend to look bigger and brighter than in the paint store or fabric shop. In kids' spaces, though, we let our typical advice go. Palettes can be as bright and bold, as fearless and fab, as your kids are.

5. Mixing Pattern and Texture

I get it. Combining a bunch of prints and patterns—not to mention textures—in a single space can be a little overwhelming. (What if they don't all go together?!?) But it doesn't have to be. Creating a layered look is all about finding the right variations of hue and scale. As I mentioned earlier, it's good to work with a lead fabric: a relatively bold textile with some nice color and a large pattern. It'll help you figure out not only your palette, but also the appropriate scale of additional prints, which should usually be more subtle. Once you have a few prints, start adding in some stripes, checks, and solids. As for texture, variation and a range of quiet and louder contrasts are your friends. You never want it to look like you got all your fabrics at once and from the same source. These tips and tricks are just the beginning. Read on for more.

When it comes to combining different prints and surfaces in a room, more is almost always better.
My favorite moment in my favorite movie, *Ferris Bueller's Day Off*, is when Ferris says, "You can never go too far." I feel that way about pattern and texture. This room goes pretty far—mixing bold chairs with the smaller pattern of the rug and the tiny print of the neutral curtains, plus sedate end chairs and art. But we could have gone even further. Ferris probably would have.

Blue and white are great. But blue and white with an accent color? Even better.

To make a blue-and-white scheme more appealing, try adding a small dose of an additional hue. Verdant shades like those here usually make an organic match for the colors of the sea and sky, especially when views through the windows include trees and other plants. Not a lot of green outside? Try combining orange, red, or yellow with blue and white.

The architect of this house called this den "The Comfort Zone," so we decorated it to live up to that name. Cushy seating and soft fabrics definitely help, but the palette does its part, too. Where low-contrast colors feel more formal, the higher contrast of the reds and blues here makes the space seem super-relaxed. Now, I just wonder why we don't name more rooms "The Comfort Zone"!

Oh, say, can you see? Red, white, and blue: They're not just for the flag anymore.

This is one of my favorite color combos. Not only is it all-American, it just feels comfy. I like to do plenty of pattern with it, to break it up a bit and make sure it doesn't look like July 4th bunting. Try to stay as close to pure, primary shades of red and blue as you can. They make the most natural combo.

When you put various striped patterns together in a room, try running them in different directions.

If I put a lot of stripes in a single space, I like to use some vertically and some horizontally. Stripes always play nicely together, so you have a lot of leeway. Here, the sheer, breezy curtains, with their side-to-side stripe, make a great backdrop for the up-and-down orientation of the pattern on the end chairs and the wainscoting.

Some rooms play with both pattern and texture, others just with one or the other—and that's perfectly fine. This family room gets its sense of style and approachable appeal from its mix of tactile materials. You just can't help wanting to reach out and touch, and then sink yourself into, the slubby linen texture of the armchair and the soft fabric of the sofa. A seagrass rug and a raffia coffee table provide welcome contrast.

A calm, serene palette and solid fabrics let a room's rich, cozy textures take center stage.

While I love mixing patterns and combining bold colors, sometimes you'll want to let texture be the star, especially in a space that's meant to be the picture of calm serenity. Here, the mix of soft and hard, smooth and rough, stands in for look-at-me hues, graphic prints, and florals.

With a low-contrast color scheme, there's nearly no end to the pattern you can pile on.
The aqua hues in this room swim across a small arc of the color wheel, from greenish to bluish. That almost-monochrome look lets you play with print with relative abandon. Here, I grounded the space with a solid sofa and rug, then mixed petite prints together, mainly on smaller items (the pillows and stools) and the curtains.

INSTANT MIX AND MATCH There's no better way to add energy and interest to a room than by layering patterns. For the best results, combine prints with a variety of different scales but related color palettes. The complementary hues help everything blend into a whole.

Pillows offer a great—and easily changeable—place for you to add pattern to a space, especially when they sit against a solid backdrop like this gray sofa. Here, two different prints in similar colors and with equally graphic looks play together nicely. They also do a good job complementing the looser lines of the curtain fabric. The scale of that print echoes the one used for the bold throw pillow.

RIGHT: Blue and green almost always work well together, whatever the specific hues. It helps, though, to pick colors of similar brightness and warmth, like those here. That ensures nothing stands out too much when all sit together.

ABOVE: Blue is great and a constant go-to color, but with a bright sofa like this one, I knew the background of the curtains had to be some other hue. The white added enough air and space to bring blue back for the accent pillow.

LEFT: When putting a small-scale print (like the one on this sofa) in front of a larger pattern (like the one used for the curtains), spend time mixing and matching the various textiles you're considering combining. If the swatches look good together, the fabrics will look even better in real life.

Whatever the room, whatever the color, when you're combining prints, remember to play with scale.
A good trick is to start with patterns that all have the same sort of palette, such as the easy blues and whites here. Next find a big, bold motif you love, like this block-print wallpaper, and then select additional patterns with diminishing scales—the medium-sized shapes of the toss pillows, the small ones of the chairs, and the teeny-tiny print on the carpet and curtains.

Even in a smaller room, big, bold prints and patterns can be your best friends.

When you don't have much square footage, your instinct might be for a very simple scheme. The right mix of patterns and a spare color palette, however, can actually *expand* close quarters. In this bedroom, the whimsical floral wallpaper and inverted Greek key curtains distract the eye, making the walls almost melt away, while solid-colored linens and nightstands provide an anchor.

Clash, shmash. Making contrasting prints, patterns, and colors work together is easier than you think.

Colors almost never clash, especially when they're different hues. The same is true of patterns, as long as you vary their scale. The room above uses a single red shade in several different ways, and with great results, but the one opposite—with all three primary hues plus green—is just as successful. The multicolored window valance, which was the palette's starting point, ties it all together.

Bold is beautiful, to be sure. In a bedroom, though, pretty prints and pale pastels are often a better way.

Subtlety brings serenity to sleep spaces, but you don't need to skip color and pattern entirely. Instead, look for low-contrast shades of barely-there hues for both solids and prints. If you like lots of pattern, use some of the larger ones on pillows or other accents. Something big used in a small way can be just enough.

If you've been thinking wallpaper doesn't make sense for your children's spaces, it's time to think again.

I've wallpapered each of my kids' rooms. It's easier to clean than painted drywall, and it lets you add artwork to all four walls. You can pick whether you want something understated or statement-making—or, if you're feeling brave, let your kids decide! What could possibly go wrong? Actually, not much.

There are no hard rules about what wallpaper goes best where, but make sure it's something you love.
Big patterns can look as great in small spaces as they do in big ones, and the opposite is true, too. The best advice I can give you about it is this: Choose a design you really like, and then just go for it. (But first, if you can, ask for as large a sample as a store can spare, to try out in your room.)

Going big with multiple bold fabric patterns is easiest when you have an otherwise blank canvas.

If you want lots of prints in a room, that's great. I'm all about it. Keep in mind, though, that the eye may need a little relief from the stimulation. You can provide that with a neutral rug and walls. These allow the patterns to do their job—which is to stand out—without competing with a complicated rug or wallpaper.

174

INSTANT SLEEP SPACES Bedrooms need to be restful, but that doesn't mean you have to keep them spare and simple. Color, pattern, and texture have a place here, too. In a primary suite, you'll want to tone the palette down, while guest rooms encourage you to try something new, and kids' spaces let you channel your children's vibe.

If a neutral palette is your pick for your primary bedroom, remember to keep the idea of mixing materials top of mind. Using several soft textures will make things interesting. Here, we've got velvet on the upholstered headboard, linen for the block-printed curtains, and high-thread-count cotton for the sheets. Grasscloth on the walls provides an additional layer and warms up the room. And because you never want too much of the same thing—not even softness—we added a mercury glass lamp and glazed mid-century nightstand.

RIGHT: No one likes crumbs in bed, but I love that this headboard fabric almost looks like confetti sprinkles on a cupcake. (Talk about sweet dreams.) The print pairs perfectly with the striped and scallop-patterned pillows.

ABOVE: In a guest room, you have more freedom to try out a color or a combination of colors that you haven't used anywhere else in your house. The various shades of grape and amethyst here, set off by the neutral walls, blend nicely.

LEFT: A headboard woven of neutral, organic materials looks just right with lighter shades of blue and green. There's something totally natural about the combination. With a woven bed, choose a nightstand of a different, smoother material.

PART THREE

THE WORKING ROOMS

Planning Makes All the Difference

Think about the hardest-working spaces in a house, and the places that spring to mind are probably the ones where you find *yourself* working the hardest: kitchens and laundry rooms, for starters, plus home offices and mudrooms. (Is there anything tougher than pulling rain-soaked boots and clothes off a toddler?) Except for kitchens—the beating heart and buzzing hub of nearly every twenty-first-century family home— these rooms tend to be afterthoughts. But we spend so much time in these spots that they deserve attention. Smart storage is key here, as are interesting wall and cabinet colors to keep things from feeling sterile, plus durable flooring and countertops. Let's take a peek at these sorts of spaces, including bathrooms, all of them as great-looking as they are hard-working.

Make your working rooms shine with painted cabinets, interesting floors, or patterned wall coverings.
Here, in a laundry room lined with smart storage from floor to ceiling, we did all three. Because we wanted the bold geometry of the porcelain-tile floor to be the hands-down "wow" factor, the walls got a print in a relatively small scale, so they wouldn't compete, and the cabinets, although painted, got a neutral gray coat.

1. Family Central: Kitchens

These days, every family I know spends most of their time at home together in the kitchen. I can't tell you how, or how long ago, this started; I just know that's the way we live now, and I love it. It means these spaces get to be warmer, more inviting, more comfortable, and more fun than they ever used to be. Kitchens are where we make our meals, but they're also where we make some of our best memories, and yes, a few big messes, too—so, you'll want to design with all that in mind. That means using durable, easy-to-clean materials; creating carefully considered work zones; and finding as much storage space as you can. It also means building the biggest island possible: That's your homework-doing, carrot-chopping, snack-eating, grocery-unpacking home base, and you'll be grateful you made it as large as you did. In these pages, we'll get into my favorite kitchen tips and tricks for cooking, entertaining, and family fun.

You know it's true, and you love it: The kitchen is the central hub and beating heart of your home.
As the place where you plan and cook meals, have cocktails, pay bills, help with schoolwork, and referee indoor soccer matches, kitchens need to function as both social *and* culinary spaces. An island is of central importance on both fronts. (I always like to have stools on two sides to avoid that lunch counter feeling.)

For kitchen floors and islands that are going to take a beating, nothing beats stained white oak.
The material is hard and just incredibly forgiving, and if you stain it in a light color, it won't show dings or chips the way painted finishes do—which makes it perfect for families. Floors, obviously, get rough treatment, and islands tend to get bumped into more than other cabinets, especially on their corners. As kids get older, islands also tend to be the site of kid (and backpack) collisions.

In eat-in kitchens, furniture and lighting help you define different zones.

A big space like this one is a blessing: You've got more than enough room for family and friends to gather around your island and your dining table during parties big or small, or just during daily dinner prep and homework sessions. But there's a challenge in making your cooking and eating spaces feel simultaneously together and apart. I like to use different light fixtures and a long bench seat whose back becomes a room divider.

Think of a kitchen's island as a piece of furniture and its tile as wallpaper.

Islands that match the rest of your kitchen cabinets are easy, but there's a missed opportunity there. I love designing islands whose turned-wood legs and stain make them look like antique sideboards or tables. Backsplashes are another place to add a feeling of real *decorating* and not just kitchen design. Details like these also help your cooking space relate to a kitchen's dining or sitting area.

For kitchens with limited sun, pick materials that help move light around.

When you've got only one window to work with—or maybe not even one—try upping the sheen of your cabinets and moldings. I typically use satin paint, but here we went with semi-gloss and a more reflective tile, which we took right up to the ceiling around the silver stove hood. By the way, don't think of the area for stools under your island as dead space: You can fit more storage here.

INSTANT KITCHEN DISPLAY Replacing upper cabinets with open shelving makes a kitchen feel much larger. Spots like these are best for dishes and glassware you need every day. If you aren't using the pieces frequently, they just tend to collect dust.

We don't want our kitchens to look like the cabinet salesperson was trying to win a commission contest by cramming in as much as humanly possible. The industrial-style shelves here, with their relatively thick surface, angled bracing, and midnight-blue color, pair naturally with the darker cabinets below. They also pop against the light backsplash tile.

RIGHT: I love white subway tiles so much that I decided we should do a whole wall of them in this kitchen, with no interruption for upper cabinets. The tiles and open shelves draw the eye up, up, up, and they beautifully frame the window, too.

ABOVE: Display shelving in a kitchen can be as deep as regular upper cabinets, letting them offer as much storage space as something enclosed. But going with narrower shelves will give your space the airiest, most open feeling.

LEFT: The homeowner who commissioned this kitchen had a very pretty collection of vintage porcelain she knew she wanted to display there. We made this nook of open shelving specifically for it. The simplicity of the all-white backdrop lets the pieces shine.

Even in an all-white kitchen, the art of the mix still very much matters.

At first, this looks like a pretty spare and simple space, which is great, because it lets it seem approachable and easygoing. But it's the room's subtle variations of texture, material, and color that make it feel lived in and alive. Nothing quite matches: You've got woven barstools, plaster walls, a glazed backsplash, and painted cabinets, and no two of the ever-so-slightly off-white hues are the same.

There is nothing more classic than a white kitchen. They never go out of style—and with good reason.
If you're having trouble choosing a palette for your kitchen, or if the idea of adding color here stresses you out, you really can't go wrong with white on white. To bring in a little bit of color—but only as much as you feel comfortable with—try doing something on your windows or counter stools.

**All-wood kitchens
are just as
eye-pleasing as
white ones, and
they're warmer, too.**

There are tons of benefits to
leaving the wood in your
kitchen unpainted. Some are
practical: The cabinets won't
show chips, dings, or dents
like painted ones would.
Others are atmospheric:
There's just something
super-cozy about wrapping a
room in natural wood grains.
Here, we capitalized on that
warmth by choosing a floor
with a similarly organic look
in a finish to match.

Where you place your appliances in a kitchen matters.
To maximize efficiency, you want your sink, range, and refrigerator pretty close to one another and located at the three corners of your "work triangle." In a room big enough for a breakfast area, adding an extra sink and warming oven or microwave near the table is always a good idea.

Even when connected, kitchens and breakfast rooms can feel like separate spaces.

To define the two different zones—cooking and eating—we partially filled the wide opening between them with lower cabinets. They suggest the feeling of a pass-through, making it easy to get food from kitchen to table, and they can serve as a buffet or sideboard, too. All the upholstery you see is faux leather or vinylized fabric (the only things I'll use in a kitchen).

To preserve big views offered by big windows, go for a small light fixture.

If you've got great views, pick a subtle pendant lamp—avoiding anything with a big drum shade—so you don't block anyone's sightlines. At my family's house, we're lucky to be able to look out over the St. Johns River from the windows in our breakfast nook. This view, plus the cozy banquette, make it the spot where everyone wants to sit.

INSTANT BANQUETTE I love banquettes not just because they look great, but also because they encourage family togetherness during meals, games, and homework time. They're super space-savers, too: A banquette means you don't need all that extra room to pull out a chair.

There is zero chance this table would have fit in this kitchen without a corner banquette. Space saving, achieved! With the bench in place, the dining area is the definition of cozy. Kids were going to be its primary occupants, so I made the wood portion lower and the cushions extra-thick. They increase the comfort factor and bring it up to the ideal seating height of seventeen inches.

RIGHT: Placing a banquette between two doors anchors it to the wall, allowing for easy traffic flow from both sides. That is especially useful here, where those doors lead to an outdoor room with a grill.

ABOVE: Corner banquettes are great, but they can be tough to get in and out of. Here, we installed a bench only under the long row of windows, not beneath the one at the foot of the table. Lots of pillows mean no one bumps into the hard edge of the windowsill.

LEFT: Not only do banquettes save floor space, they also let more people fit comfortably around a table, especially a smaller one like this. In addition, they give you more room to play with interesting table bases, because there are fewer chair legs getting in the way.

2. Private Spaces: Bathrooms

I'll never forget the first time I got up in the middle of the night to take my older son—then a toddler in the later stages of potty training—to the bathroom. I was bumping around, bleary-eyed, trying to help him get from his bed to the toilet. Once there, firmly enthroned, he asked for a magazine . . . and then told me to scram. And who could blame him? If positions were reversed, I'd have done the same thing. We like our privacy and our comfort, and from an early age, too. That's a lesson to carry with you as you think about designing your own bathrooms, which may have limited space or natural light, or other constraints. What can you do to make a powder room or guest bath comfortable yet playful? How do you insert a spa-like atmosphere into a primary suite? What do your kids need from their bathroom, and how do you ensure that space will grow up with them? I don't have *all* the answers, but you'll find quite a few solutions to these riddles here.

When you can spare the space, a wet room is a bathroom must-have in a family home.
I've become more and more of a fan of these sorts of all-in-one bathing zones, with a big soaking tub included behind the glass doors of a shower. No need to worry about kids (or spouses) splashing water all over the place when the whole thing is tiled, with a central floor drain.

Playing with unexpected materials—or with expected materials in unexpected ways—adds personality.

It's easy for bathrooms to look cookie cutter. Mixing woods is a great way to prevent that from happening. Mahogany, like that used above, is great because it's incredibly durable and offers a nautical look. The white linen cabinet breaks up the dark stain. OPPOSITE: The undulating shape of a plaster mirror offers contrast to this bathroom's straight lines and smooth surfaces.

Because they're often short on space and accessories, wallpaper is one of the best ways to bring a bathroom to life.
Wallpapering a bathroom—whether with a bold or more subtle design—is an all-around win. The first benefit is that nothing has as big a visual impact. Secondly, it's cost effective because these spaces have relatively little wall space. And third off, it's simple to keep clean, since most wallpaper is easily washable.

Bathrooms for children need to be functional—but they can be fun and even a little fab, too.

Your kids, like mine, can likely take a clean sink and turn it into a mud pit in no time. So it's tempting to say "why bother?" about their bathrooms. But I've found that creating a great-looking space can actually encourage them to keep it neat. At least sometimes. OPPOSITE: A trough sink with three faucets is just right for a family with a trio of sons. An added bonus? There's no countertop for the little guys to get dirty.

Aqua is almost always a safe pick for the palette of your bathroom. (It's called a water closet, after all.)

Here we've got aqua done two ways. Above, the vanity matches the walls, for a monochrome, cohesive look. Opposite, the white vanity creates a more relaxed atmosphere—you might even call it spa-like. This room has a large linen closet and a second vanity, too, and doing a color for all that cabinetry seemed like too much.

INSTANT POWDER ROOM PIZZAZZ Half baths tend to be short on square footage—if they weren't, they probably would've been full baths, right? To make the most of these tight spaces, use pattern and color to your advantage, look for creative storage, and go custom whenever you can.

Hand-blocked wallpaper really brings this room to life. With a statement-making pattern like this, don't distract from it with any other fussy, or even complex, details. We chose a simple marble-topped wooden vanity with open storage below—the better to create a sense of space in this teeny-tiny room tucked under a staircase.

RIGHT: In this powder room with a low ceiling, we ran the rectangular tiles vertically to make the space seem as tall as possible. The mottled glazing, which looks like marble or water, creates a stunning backdrop.

ABOVE: A diminutive powder room is *the* place to use a big, bold wallpaper you love but might be scared to put in a spot that's busier or has more walls. A pattern like this saves a small room from feeling bare or cold.

LEFT: A custom-shaped countertop with a bump out in the middle allowed this room to have a more generously sized sink. The space is so small, the door would have hit the side of the marble if we hadn't reduced the depth on the sides.

3. A Place for Everything: Storage

You can never have enough storage. Even if you think you're designing more than you need, I can guarantee you, you're not. (If nothing else, unused lower cabinets make great hiding spots for pick-up games of hide-and-seek with the kids.) These days, storage isn't just for closets, basements, attics, and other places no one else but you ever sees—and it goes beyond mudrooms and laundry rooms, too, to include home offices and even bedrooms. Because of that, the best twenty-first-century storage solutions aren't just smart, they're attractive, too. Think of your laundry room as a kitchen in miniature and your mudrooms as user-friendly closets turned inside out. It's easy to design these spaces so they become rooms you'll *want* to spend time in rather than places you *have* to be chained to—even if you're trying to match your hundredth pair of athletic socks or fishing around the backs of drawers looking for lost toys.

No matter what you do, you won't ever have enough space to put everything away. And that's OK.
When we moved into our house, we thought we had designed in so much extra storage, but in the blink of an eye, it was gone. If you build it, you'll fill it, trust me. That's why it's so important to cover the walls of working rooms with as many drawers and cabinets as you possibly can. You won't regret it later.

Decorate your laundry room like it's a small kitchen. You're going to spend a ton of time there.
Every parent of young children knows there's no keeping up with the piles of dirty clothes. Treat yourself to a space that'll take some of the pain out of the stain-scrubbing, folding, and ironing. This room, designed for a family with pets, is used for dog-bathing, too. The painted wainscoting prevents scratches to the wallpaper above.

220

**You don't need a butler to have a butler's pantry.
These rooms are a dream for storage and serving.**

The best ones feature a wine fridge, small sink, tons of counterspace, and cabinets
from floor to ceiling. OPPOSITE: Create your own custom-height washer and dryer
stand, with storage below, to match your cabinetry. Put a durable countertop material
on top if you're worried about leaks from the bottom of the machines.

Never be afraid to use bold color in a small space—especially if it's designed for grunt work.

There's no better place for bright hues than a room where you're going to be working away thanklessly: doing laundry, making your way through paperwork, and paying bills. The worst. I can't say good design can make it all better, and it certainly won't make it all go away, but it sure makes it more tolerable.

The secret to making a home office seem more warm and welcoming? Do what you can to hide your desk.

Or at least stick it off to the side and keep it small. Almost gone are the days of the grand desk front and center, with a big computer on top. Now, most of our work is done from a comfy chair or sofa on our laptops. Lean in to that idea. Oh, and if you've got nice books, open shelves are great; otherwise, go for cabinets with doors.

INSTANT HOME OFFICE There's no such thing as a one-size-fits-all work space. I'm a pacer; I do best moving around. But that doesn't mean *you* shouldn't have a desk. To make working at home easier and more pleasurable, you need to tailor-make a room that helps you get your job done the way you want to.

The scheme here sprang out of the great color in the homeowner's artwork. That piece led to the idea of painting the cabinet underneath to also look like a modernist abstraction, albeit a much more geometric one. The seafoam-colored wallpaper creates a soothing, neutral backdrop, while the pale, clean-lined desk and chairs relate to the modern art without distracting from it.

RIGHT: This is a working office used forty hours a week—but you'd never know it. The cabinets and drawers conceal books, papers, a printer, and more. Just what we messy types need! We picked light blue to match the sky outside and the darker blue tulip print to contrast with it.

ABOVE: We could spare only the shallowest space for a built-in desk in this study. To add depth, we found a three-dimensional wall covering made of small, geometric wood panels, then painted the cabinetry and desk a contrasting but soothing slate blue.

LEFT: A bedroom homework zone works perfectly for the active teenager we designed it for. The layers of bold pattern and various verdant shades could have been too much, but they proved just the thing for a girl who's over the moon for the color green.

Color can make storage solutions look like the height of fashion—and the furthest thing from utilitarian.

I avoid white cabinets outside of kitchens and primary bathrooms, so I loved this homeowner's request for a Tiffany blue closet. I always like to include a spot to sit to put shoes on, like the window seat here. OPPOSITE: When you have a bedroom without a closet, try building the storage around the headboard. It creates a cozy recess.

Bespoke bunk beds become organizational lifesavers when they do double duty as storage centers.

Let's face it: In kids' rooms, you're never going to have enough spots to stow all that junk. Built-in bunk beds provide tons of opportunities for hidden drawers. Try putting them in the lower mattress platforms and in the stairs up to the top bunk above, too.

INSTANT MUDROOM If you're like me, you have a love-hate relationship with mudrooms. We love having a place for the endless stuff that comes with busy family life but hate that there's never quite enough room for it all. Even when there's stuff spillover, however, your mudroom can still look great.

Think of your mudroom as a drop zone—a perfect place for backpacks, shoes, soccer balls, and anything else that belongs halfway between indoors and out, or between the garage and the rest of the house. Hanging spaces are super-important for getting things off the usually less-than-perfectly-clean floor (they're called *mudrooms* for a reason), as are places to sit. Sometimes, a few hooks and a freestanding bench are all it takes; wallpaper never hurts, either.

RIGHT: Mudrooms work best with durable flooring (preferably porcelain tile) and some interesting color. In a mostly neutral scheme, a bright hue can make a big difference, even when used in a small way. And if you get tired of the accent wall, a change is just a coat of paint away.

ABOVE: In this mudroom, we kept the cabinetry all one hue instead of adding an accent color. That lets the graphic, geometric pattern of the cement-tile floor command attention, with no unnecessary distractions.

LEFT: Surfboard wallpaper tells you you're walking into a beach house—and that this spot is sandier than it is muddy. More than anywhere else, a home on the coast needs this sort of space, one outfitted with tough, water-resistant (but still great looking) finishes and fabrics.

A place for everything doesn't mean that everything always *has* to be in its place.

But at least it leaves open the possibility that it can be sometimes! These books and toys probably spend way more time on the floor, tucked behind the armchair cushions, and strewn across that craft table than they do neatly arrayed on the shelves. Even so, what parent wouldn't want a storage wall like this?

About the Author

Almost two decades ago, I walked into a design store for an interview and walked out with a job that would change my life. It was my parents' shop, after all. As it turns out, a love for beautiful homes and happy people is in my blood, and I've been doing my best to nurture that ever since. It's not always paint swatches and mattress testing (I had no idea the time and amount of learning required to be successful in this business!), but I'm still excited to be here, all these years later. Passion is key in design, and I'm lucky to feel more and more passionate about what I do each day.

It's an honor to help people give shape to their dreams, even while I'm still working on some of my own—I'm positive that if I was just one foot taller and a lot more coordinated, I could have easily made it as a professional golfer. And while it's not exactly the same as wearing that green jacket, I was thrilled to be named by *House Beautiful* and *Traditional Home* as one of the Top Young Designers in America a few years ago. I was also named one of Sotheby's Top 20 Designers in America in 2020. My work has also been featured in *Veranda*, *House Beautiful*, *Traditional Home*, *Southern Living*, *Coastal Living*, *Country Living*, *Atlanta Homes & Lifestyles*, and *Luxe*.

Somewhere along the way, I also managed to marry a wonderful woman and have two fantastic sons (who even afford me a decent night's sleep every now and then). Every day I am fortunate to work with great clients and a very talented staff. My goal as a designer is the same today as it was from day one: I want to create spaces with longevity that properly reflect my clients' personal styles and that can be enjoyed by everyone.

— andrewjhoward.com / @andrewjhow

Acknowledgments

Too often, we designers lucky enough to have our names on our firm's front door get all the credit for our projects, even though the work is always a majorly collaborative effort. I've had the great good fortune to team up with an amazing group of young designers over the years, folks who've poured their hearts and souls into making the houses we decorate look their best. Special thanks go to my studio right-hands, Kelsey Heneveld, Lindsey Braren, Lindsey Waters, and Meg Hickey. Without your incredible design sense, none of what's in this book would have been possible. (And without your courtesy laughing at my jokes, it's possible no one would laugh at them at all.)

I'm one of those people lucky enough to have two sets of parents, and I would like to thank both of them. My dad, Jim, and Phoebe, designers themselves, taught me everything I needed to know about the field, both aesthetically and business-wise, and were patient with me when I asked lots of questions in the early days. My mom, Carol, and Ed, meanwhile, taught me the importance of treating everyone with kindness and respect, even when it was not easy.

Every homeowner I have worked with has entrusted me to help them with their house, and for that I am grateful. Getting to know each of you personally was always just as much fun as working on your projects together, and the pleasure of the laughs and good times we shared will always outweigh the pain of last-minute deliveries that seemed like they would never make it on time.

I have worked with countless architects and builders over the years—too many to name here, but most notably Kevin Gray and Cronk Duch. You all have pushed me to become a better designer, and I enjoy each new collaboration more than the one before.

To the photographers and stylists who have been on shoots with me, I say thank you for your incredible work to show my designs in the most wonderful light possible. The styling skills of Frances Bailey, Heather Chadduck Hillegas, Helen Crowther, Elizabeth Demos, Doretta Sperduto, and Liz Strong are matched only by the camera talents of Lucas Allen, Brittany Ambridge, Zach DeSart, Laurey Glenn, Max Kim-Bee, Francesco Lagnese, David A. Land, Helen Norman, Eric Piasecki, Chris Shane, David Tsay, and Stacey Van Berkel. You made each image in this book memorable.

Book designer Doug Turshen and his professional partner Steve Turner, as well as Shawna Mullen and the whole team at Abrams, believed in my work enough to help conceive this book and then see it through to publication. You're the best. Writer and editor Andrew Sessa (my brother from another mother) was able to capture my voice in a way that I never thought possible—and he listened to enough stories about my kids to put almost any normal human to sleep.

Last but not least, thanks to God for giving me an amazing family and the ability to do a job I love. My wife, Katie, and our sons, Jack and Henry, have taught me more about decorating and life than any project ever will. From Katie, I learned the importance of patience, and our kids have shown me how necessary it is to create houses and spaces that are actually comfortable to live in and not just lovely to look at. The three of them have supported me in the best of times and the worst, and they've let me stick around even though I've forced them to look at more design photos than any human ever should.

To end, this quote from Bishop Jeremy Taylor describes my feelings on family more accurately than I ever could: "Marriage (and family) hath in it less beauty but more of safety than the single life; it hath more care, but less danger, it is more merry, and more sad; it is fuller of sorrows and fuller of joys; it lies under more burdens, but it is supported by all the strengths of love and charity, and those burdens are delightful."

Photo Credits

Helen Norman 2–3, 98, 156, 164–165

Brittany Ambridge 5, 116–117, 126

Eric Piasecki 6, 11, 23, 28–29, 96, 97, 102–103, 114–115, 141 (bottom), 144–145, 158–159, 161 (bottom right), 162, 163, 166, 167, 184–185, 186, 187, 200–201, 210, 217 (left), 220–221

Francesco Lagnese 8, 32–33, 122–123, 170, 171, 181, 226, 227

Max Kim–Bee 12, 38–39, 41, 46–47, 49, 58–59, 60–61, 64, 65, 78–79, 84, 85, 108–109, 112, 118, 120–121, 125 (top left), 130–131, 139, 143, 168, 195, 196–197, 198–199, 202–203, 204, 205 (bottom), 211 (left), 214, 215, 216, 223, 232, 235 (left), 236–237

David Tsay 15, 18–19, 24–25, 26–27, 48, 110–111, 128, 129, 140, 150–151, 178, 205 (top right), 206, 219, 229 (left), 231

Lucas Allen 16–17, 20–21, 36–37, 51, 70–71, 72, 76–77, 81, 82–83, 94, 95, 99, 100, 105 (top left), 107, 136, 137, 146, 176, 208, 209, 212, 222, 229 (top and bottom right)

Laurey Glenn 30, 34, 35, 52–53, 54, 55, 62–63, 68, 86, 92–93, 105 (bottom), 113, 135, 138, 141 (top right), 160, 161 (top right), 174–175, 177 (all), 190, 192–193, 205 (left), 224–225

David Land 42–43, 73, 74–75, 88–89, 91, 104, 105 (top right), 119, 124, 125 (top right and bottom), 132, 133, 141 (left), 142, 149, 169, 172, 182, 183, 191 (top right), 194, 211 (right), 213, 217 (top right, bottom right), 228, 230, 233, 234, 235 (bottom right), 238

Chris Shane 44–45, 152–153, 161 (left), 191 (left)

Zach Desart 56–57, 67, 101, 147, 173, 235 (top right)

Stacey Van Berkel 154–155, 188–189, 191 (bottom)

Editor: Shawna Mullen
Designer: Doug Turshen with Steve Turner
Production Manager: Larry Pekarek

Library of Congress Control Number: 2021932559

ISBN: 978-1-4197-5276-6
eISBN: 978-1-64700-217-6

Text copyright © 2021 Andrew Howard

Cover © 2021 Abrams

Printed and bound in China
10 9 8 7 6 5 4 3 2 1

Abrams books are available at special discounts when purchased in quantity for premiums and promotions as well as fundraising or educational use. Special editions can also be created to specification. For details, contact specialsales@abramsbooks.com or the address below.

Abrams® is a registered trademark of Harry N. Abrams, Inc.

ABRAMS The Art of Books
195 Broadway, New York, NY 10007
abramsbooks.com

195 Broadway
New York, NY 10007
abramsbooks.com